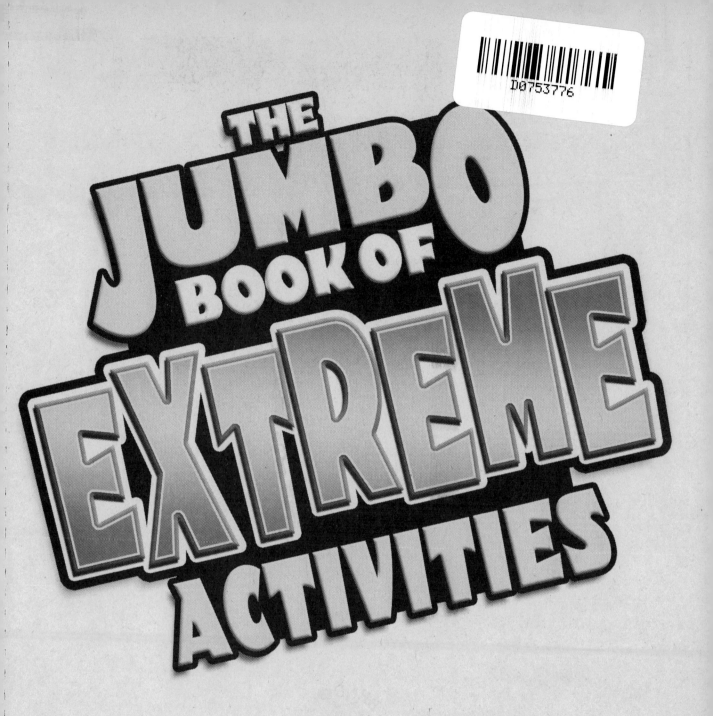

THE JUMBO BOOK OF EXTREME ACTIVITIES

BY
TONY TALLARICO

Bendon Publishing International, Inc.
Ashland, OH 44805
www.bendonpub.com

Visit us at www.bendonpub.com

INTRODUCTION

Are you ready for some **JUMBO** fun? Hours and hours of challenging fun and games are just ahead.

There's never a dull moment with these cool activities designed especially to sharpen your solving skills. **THE JUMBO BOOK OF EXTREME ACTIVITIES** is jam-packed with mazes, hidden pictures, drawing fun, secret codes, crosswords, word games, picture puzzles, and much, much more!

So what are you waiting for? Grab a pencil, turn the page, and step inside the **JUMBO** world of extreme activities!

(Answers begin on page 79.)

WORD WALL

Fill in this wall by using the letters in the top word—**EGG**—to complete the other words. Some letters may be used more than once in a word.

	E	G	G		
B	I				R
	A	R	A		
T	A				D
W	I			L	
	I			L	
	A	R		L	
		T	T	I	N
		O	L	O		Y
	L	O	R		O	U	S
L				I	N		S
	R		T		I	N	

STATE MAZE

Follow the path to the capital of the state of **ARKANSAS**.

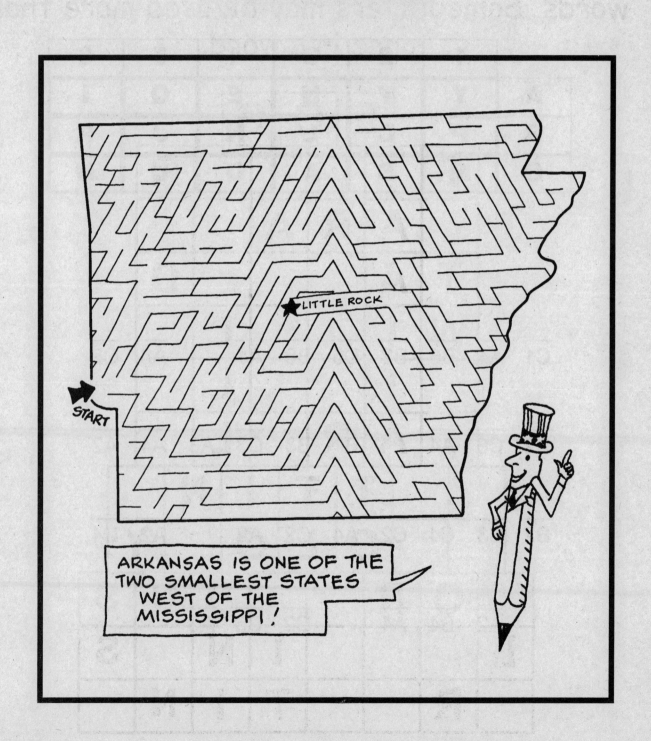

LITTLE ROCK

START

ARKANSAS IS ONE OF THE TWO SMALLEST STATES WEST OF THE MISSISSIPPI!

LET'S DECODE

Use the chart below to decode this cosmic fact.

	1	2	3	4	5	6
A	Y	T	N	E	Q	I
B	P	C	L	H	J	R
C	M	S	A	O	U	H

C1 A4 B6 B2 C5 B6 A1   A6 C2

A2 C6 A4   B1 B3 C3 A3 A4 A2

B2 B3 C4 C2 A4 C2 A2   A2 C4

A2 B4 A4   C2 C5 A3 .

REBUS FUN

Solve this rebus puzzle.

= _ _ _ _ _ _ _ _ _ _ _ '

FIRST LADY FIRST

Do you know which president's wife was the first to introduce ice cream at White House functions? Choose and follow the path made up only of letters from the words

ICE CREAM

to learn the correct answer.

(Move horizontally and vertically only.)

start
↓

C	M	R	E	P	T	I	B	F	G	C	R	M	E
K	L	J	H	Y	R	C	M	E	Q	U	O	P	N
V	X	I	C	E	H	B	D	R	I	T	Q	Y	Y
Z	M	K	J	S	V	T	S	A	P	L	O	N	T
R	E	A	ABIGAIL ADAMS			X	M	E	M	I	R	C
P	P	T				Q	P	L	N	B	V	C
C	V	B	N	H	Y	T	F	D	S	Q	P	X	A
R	M	A	E	I	C	R	M	K	L	P	S	T	M
I	Y	U	N	B	X	R	Q	T	S	T	Y	I	I
M	M	N	B	V	X	T	DOLLEY MADISON			S	S	C
P	L	O	K	J	L	N				N	T	E
Q	MARTHA WASHINGTON			T	T	S	P	M	P	Q	Z	A
E				P	E	I	R	C	P	L	T	R
A	M	U	T	S	L	C	L	S	T	Q	E	A	M
M	E	A	R	C	T	R	M	R	C	I	I	Y	Q

8

SEARCH & FIND®

ICE HOCKEY MADNESS

- ☐ car
- ☐ cat
- ☐ clown
- ☐ fishing pole
- ☐☐ hockey pucks
- ☐ in-line skate
- ☐ mitten
- ☐ paintbrush
- ☐ pencil
- ☐ sailboat
- ☐ star
- ☐ toothbrush
- ☐ violin

THINGS THAT ARE DIFFERENT

Can you find and circle **8** things that are different between these two pictures?

A DIFFERENT ORDER

Sometimes the letters of a word can be placed in a different order to spell a new word. An example of this would be changing **LAST** into **SALT**. Draw a line from each word on the left to its new word on the right.

EARN	MOAT
DEN	MEAL
ATOM	RIDE
BAT	END
MALE	PART
DIRE	TAB
CAR	ARC
TRAP	DRAW
WARD	TAP
PAT	NEAR

WHAT'S WRONG HERE?

Can you find and circle **20** things that are wrong or just don't belong here?

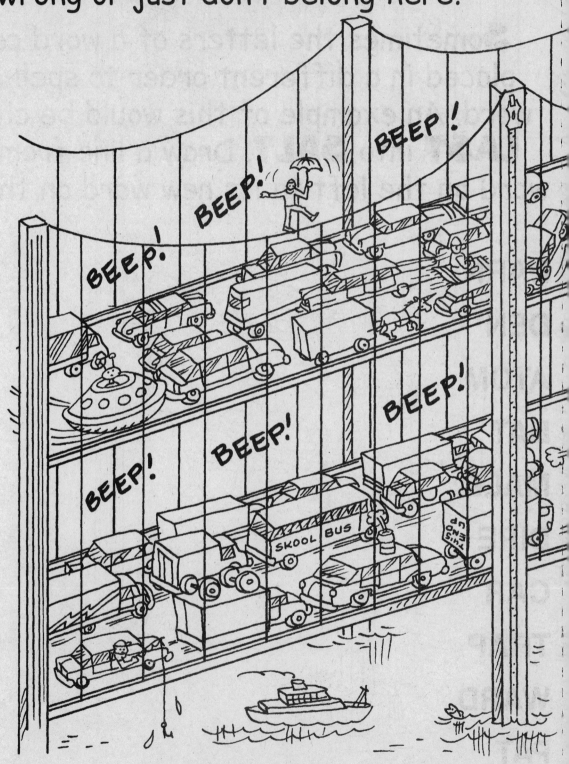

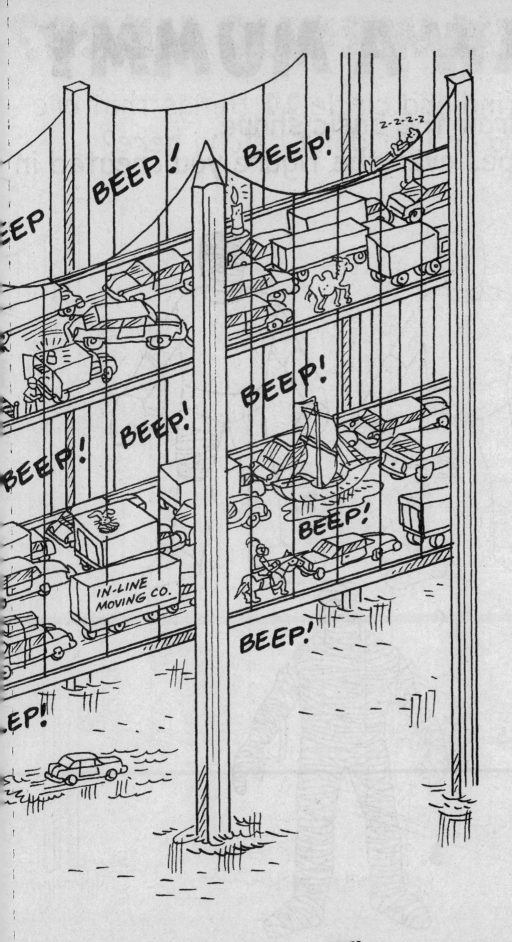

DRAW A MUMMY

1. Lightly draw the basic shape.
2. Add shapes over the figure you created in step #1.

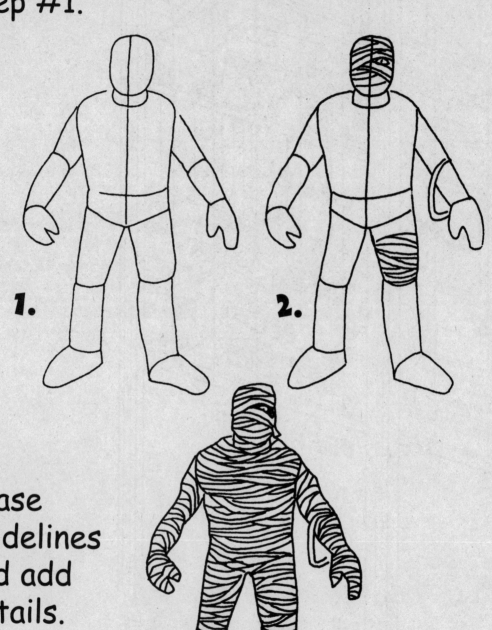

1.

2.

3. Erase guidelines and add details.

3.

Draw your mummy here.

WORD-PIX

Find and circle a picture that represents each of the following words or phrases in this very wacky scene.

BLOCKHEAD ✦ HEAVY-HANDED ✦ HORSESHOES
SMALL TALK ✦ WALKING STICK

HOMONYM FUN

Homonyms are words that sound the same but are spelled differently and have different meanings (like **REAL** and **REEL**). Choose and circle the correct word for each sentence.

1. Your eyes enable you to **SEA** or **SEE**.

2. A vegetable related to the onion is a **LEEK** or **LEAK**.

3. A preserve made of fruit is called **JAM** or **JAMB**.

4. You wear sneakers on your **FEET** or **FEAT**.

5. A fruit with a rounded base is a **PEAR** or **PAIR**.

6. A part in a play is called a **ROLL** or **ROLE**.

PICTURE CROSSWORD

Across

Down

FAMILY WORD SEARCH

AUNT ✦ BROTHER ✦ OUSIN ✦ DADDY ✦ FATHER
GRANDMA ✦ GRANDPA ✦ MOMMY ✦ MOTHER
NIECE ✦ RELATIVE ✦ SISTER ✦ UNCLE

```
D R E T S I S H F
A N V U N C L E A
D G I C M T E N T
D R T M O M M Y H
Y A A A T U W T E
T N L H H J S R R
R D E C E I N I T
C P R A R Y C M N
E A M D N A R G U
B R O T H E R R A
```

MYSTERY PICTURE

Draw exactly what you see in the numbered boxes at the top into the blank boxes of the same number below.

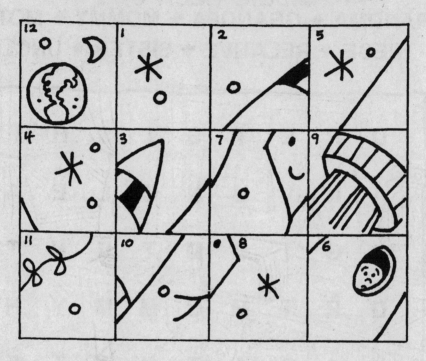

1	2	3	4
5	6	7	8
9	10	11	12

ON THE LOOKOUT

How many things can you find in this scene
that begin with the letter **T**?
Circle each one.

DROP A LETTER

Drop a letter from every word in column **A** to form a new word in column **B**. Write each dropped letter in column **C** to form the name of a popular water sport.

A	B	C
NEST		
OUR		
HER		
SIFT		
RAIN		
NONE		
GROW		

DECODE-A-JOKE

The chart to the left contains all the letters you will need to decode this musical joke.

A=14
C=9
D=11
E=6
F=16
H=2
I=13
K=7
M=5
N=12
O=3
P=10
S=1
T=15
U=8
W=4
X=17

$\underline{4}\ \underline{2}\ \underline{14}\ \underline{15}\qquad \underline{7}\ \underline{13}\ \underline{12}\ \underline{11}$

$\underline{3}\ \underline{16}\qquad \underline{10}\ \underline{2}\ \underline{3}\ \underline{12}\ \underline{6}$

$\underline{9}\ \underline{14}\ \underline{12}\qquad \underline{5}\ \underline{14}\ \underline{7}\ \underline{6}$

$\underline{5}\ \underline{8}\ \underline{1}\ \underline{13}\ \underline{9}$?

$\underline{14}$

$\underline{1}\ \underline{14}\ \underline{17}\ \underline{3}\ \underline{10}\ \underline{2}\ \underline{3}\ \underline{12}\ \underline{6}$!

HA-HA-HA- -HA-HA- HA-HA-HA!

LOOK ALIKE?

Can you find and circle at least **10** things that are different between these two pictures?

LADDER CROSSWORD

1. Large boat
2. Tropical bird
3. A group of three
4. Strange or unusual
5. Percussion instrument
6. Moo juice
7. A set of parts
8. Short for Timothy

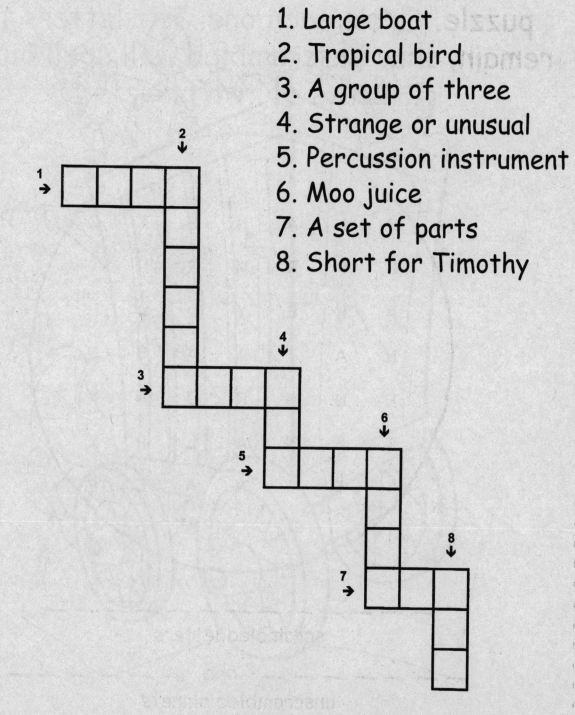

SCRAMBLED MYSTERY PLANETS

The word **PLANET** appears **7** times in this puzzle. Circle each one. The letters that remain, once unscrambled, will spell out the names of two planets.

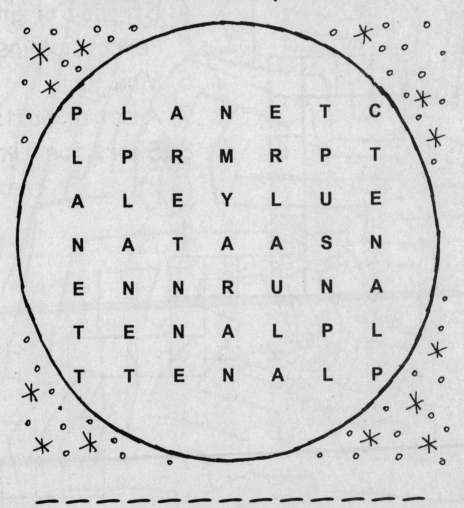

```
P  L  A  N  E  T  C
L  P  R  M  R  P  T
A  L  E  Y  L  U  E
N  A  T  A  A  S  N
E  N  N  R  U  N  A
T  E  N  A  L  P  L
T  T  E  N  A  L  P
```

_ _ _ _ _ _ _ _ _ _ _ _ _ _ _ _ _ _ _

scrambled letters

_ _ _ _ _ _ _ _ _ _ and _ _ _ _ _ _

unscrambled planets

BASKETBALL MAZE

Score the winning basket.

SEARCH & FIND®

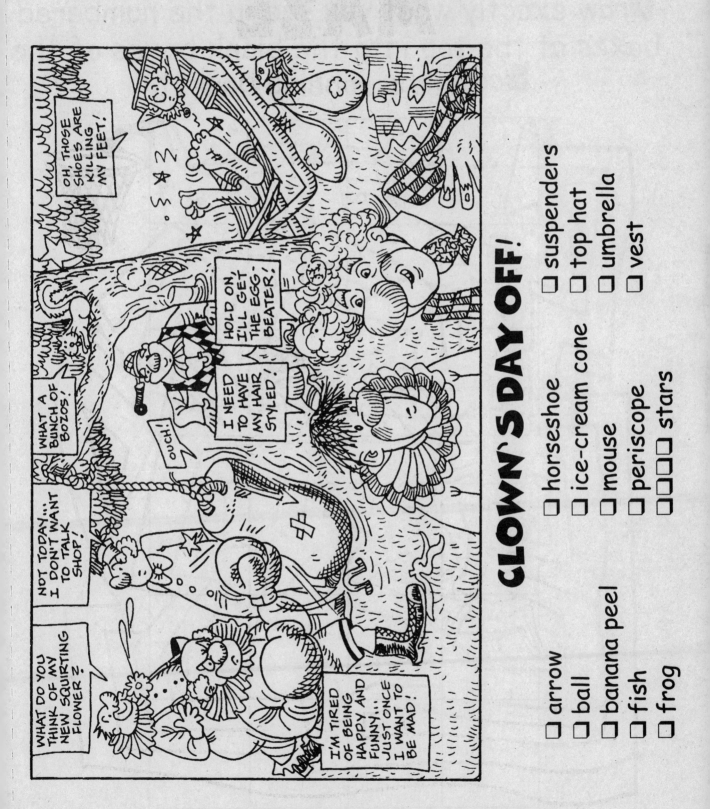

CLOWN'S DAY OFF!

- ☐ arrow
- ☐ ball
- ☐ banana peel
- ☐ fish
- ☐ frog
- ☐ horseshoe
- ☐ ice-cream cone
- ☐ mouse
- ☐ periscope
- ☐☐☐ stars
- ☐ suspenders
- ☐ top hat
- ☐ umbrella
- ☐ vest

MYSTERY PICTURE

Draw exactly what you see in the numbered boxes at the top into the blank boxes of the same number below.

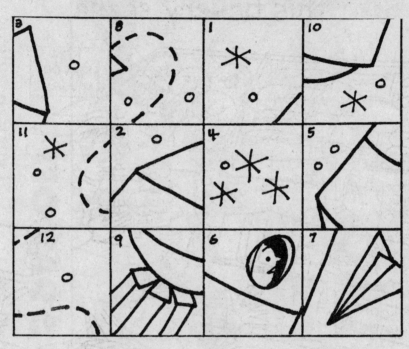

WHAT'S WRONG HERE?

Find and circle **10** things that are wrong in this bakery scene.

LET'S SPELL

Write the name of each object pictured. The letters that fall into the squares will spell out the name of a U.S. state.

PIX WORD SEARCH

Find and circle the names of these objects in this word-search puzzle.

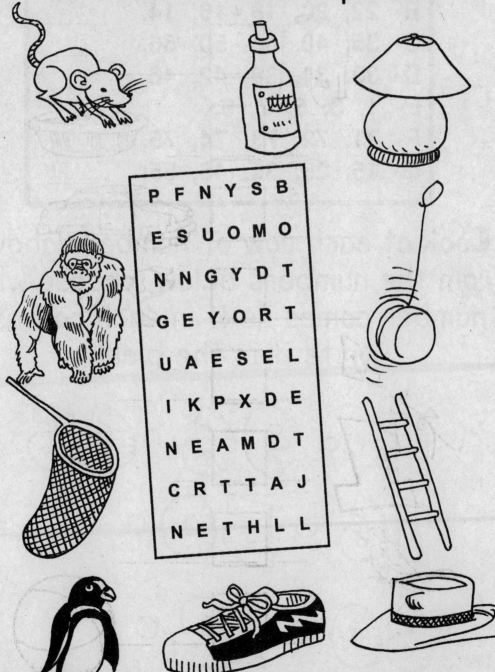

```
P F N Y S B
E S U O M O
N N G Y D T
G E Y O R T
U A E S E L
I K P X D E
N E A M D T
C R T T A J
N E T H L L
```

PLAY BY THE NUMBERS

A- 3, 6, 12, 24, 48, ____
B- 22, 20, 18, 16, 14, ____
C- 35, 40, 45, 50, 55, ____
D- 30, 34, 38, 42, 46, ____
E- 1, 3, 5, 7, 9, ____
F- 71, 72, 73, 74, 75, ____
G- 15, 25, 35, 45, 55, ____

Look at each row of numbers above. From the numbers below, choose which number comes next in each row and write it in the blank.

11 ∘ 96 ∘ 65 ∘
16 ∘ 50 ∘
60 ∘ 12 ∘

BULL'S-EYE MAZE

Hit the target!

DRAW A CAT NAMED CHIX

1. Lightly draw the basic shapes.
2. Add shapes over the figure you created in step #1.

1.

2.

3.

3. Erase guidelines and add details.

Draw Chix here.

DID YOU KNOW?

Unscramble and complete this historical fact by writing the letter of the alphabet that comes BEFORE each of these letters.

U I F   B O D J F O U

D J U Z   P G

Q P N Q F J J '   J U B M Z '

X B T   C V S J F E

V O E F S   B T I   B O E

S P D L   X I F O   U I F

W P M D B O P

N U .   W F T V W J V T

ERUPTED IN 79 A.D.

UNCLE SAM'S PUZZLE

How many times does the word **LIBERTY** appear? Uncle Sam wants you to circle and count each one!

```
Y Y T R E B I L
L I B E Y Y Y I
L I B R T T Y B
I T B T R T Y E
B Y B E R T Y R
E T B T R E B T
R I B I R T Y Y
L I B E R T Y Y
```

TOTAL: _____

39

WHICH FOUR?

Do you know which four U.S. presidents are carved into the Mount Rushmore National Memorial in South Dakota? Choose and follow the path made up only of letters from the words **MOUNT RUSHMORE** to learn the correct answer.

(Move horizontally and vertically only.)

start
⇓

M	N	T	R	S	E	U	H	Q
W	Y	I	P	A	D	F	T	J
O	E	GEORGE WASHINGTON THOMAS JEFFERSON				K	O	L
M	Z	TEDDY ROOSEVELT ABRAHAM LINCOLN				X	M	C
S	V	B	M	N	Q	W	U	Y
H	I	A	P	D	F	R	S	G
R	GEORGE WASHINGTON JOHN ADAMS				J	E	L	K
E	TEDDY ROOSEVELT ABRAHAM LINCOLN				X	T	N	W
T	A	B	V	C	P	Q	H	Z
N	Y	D	N	T	U	O	M	D
U	L	K	R	A	X	B	C	Y
O	I	K	S	I	GEORGE WASHINGTON THOMAS JEFFERSON			
N	J	A	U	A	FRANKLIN ROOSEVELT ABRAHAM LINCOLN			
H	M	S	N	Q	W	M	N	E

SEARCH & FIND®

CURIOUS KIDS

- apple
- bare foot
- crumpled-up paper
- eyeglasses
- fish
- flower
- football
- graduation cap
- hot dog
- kite
- open book
- paintbrush
- pencil
- ruler
- tack

DECODE-A-RIDDLE

The chart below contains all the letters you will need to decode this riddle.

A=7	C=14	D=1	E=11	F=5	H=9
I=18	K=3	L=15	M=12	N=8	O=17
R=4	S=10	T=16	U=2	W=13	Y=6

W H A T   I S   T H E
13 9 7 16   18 10   16 9 11

M O S T
12 17 10 16

D I F F I C U L T
1 18 5 5 18 14 2 15 16

K E Y   T O   T U R N ?
3 11 6   16 17   16 2 4 8

A
7

D O N K E Y !
1 17 8 3 11 6

REBUS FUN

Solve the Christmas rebus puzzle.

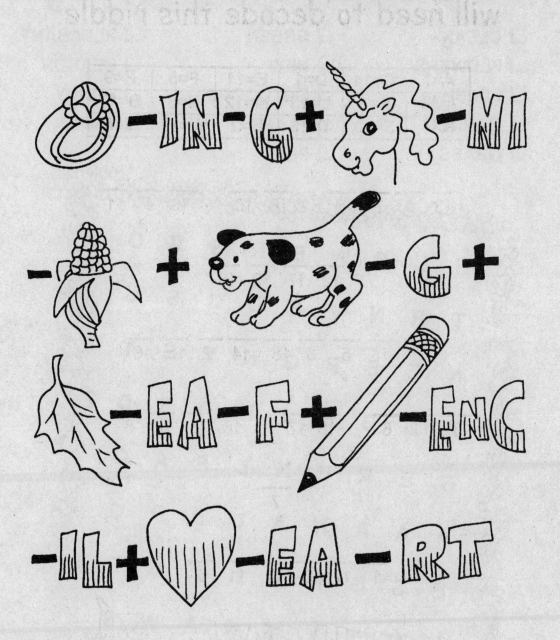

= _ _ _ _ _ _ _ _

SPRING
WORD SEARCH

- ❑ CLEAN
- ❑ FLOWERS
- ❑ FRESH
- ❑ GARDEN
- ❑ GRASS
- ❑ GREEN
- ❑ NEW
- ❑ OUTDOORS
- ❑ PLANT
- ❑ PLAY
- ❑ PLEASANT
- ❑ SEASON
- ❑ SUNNY
- ❑ WARM

```
F L O W E R S V O
T R N V E D J S U
N E E R G N Y S T
A S D S J K P S D
S E R U H L P A O
A A A N A L D R O
E S G N A L E G R
L O T Y M R A W S
P N A E L C B P Z
```

STATE MAZE

Follow the path to the capital of the state of **MISSOURI**.

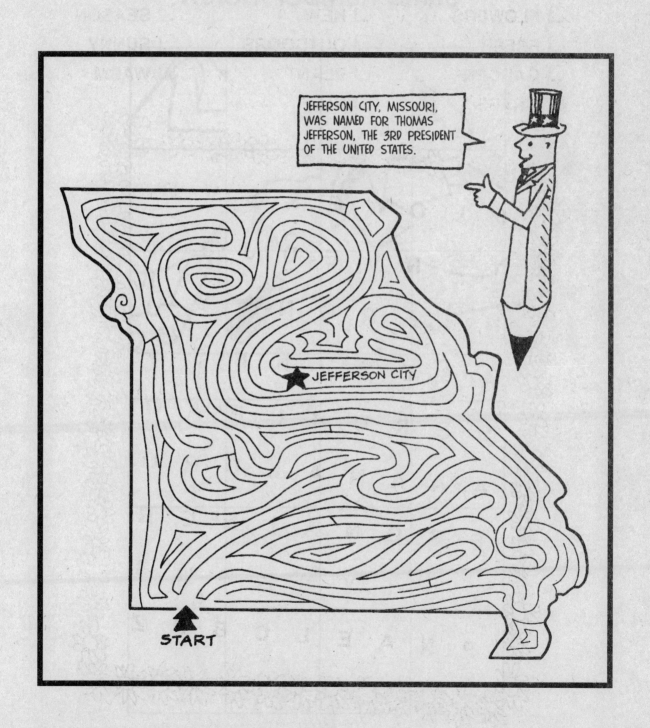

MYSTERY PICTURE

Draw exactly what you see in the numbered boxes at the top into the blank boxes of the same number below.

FIND AND CIRCLE

Find and circle **9** birds hiding
in this picture.

FORMING WORDS

Can you form at least **40** words using the letters from the word
TREASURE?

MYSTERY SENTENCE

Correctly answer each clue. Then write the numbered letters in their correct spaces below to complete the mystery sentence.

✦ Sport played on a court

    __ __ __ __ __ __ __
    18 12 13   6   1

✦ Medical expert   __ __ __ __ __ __
               4   7   17

✦ Opposite of over   __ __ __ __ __ __
                  14 9 11   20

✦ Long-necked mammal   __ __ __ __ __ __ __ __
                      5 3   10   16

✦ Spring month   __ __ __ __ __
          8 15 2 19

THE FIRST __ __ __ __ __ __ TO __ __ __ __ __ __
            1 2 3 4 5 6   7 8 9 10 11 12

WAS A __ __ S __ __ N S I __ N BRIDGE
      13 14   15 16   17

__UILT FROM N __ AGA __ A FALLS, NEW YORK.
18   19   20

TWO WORDS IN ONE

These mixed-up letters are really two words in one. Let the clues help you find them. Hint: The letters are in the correct order—the two words are just combined! The first one has been done for you.

1. PHCOTAOGRAMPHERERA
He'll snap your picture—with this.
PHOTOGRAPHER—CAMERA
‾ ‾ ‾ ‾ ‾ ‾ ‾ ‾ ‾ ‾ ‾ ‾   ‾ ‾ ‾ ‾ ‾ ‾

2. AMOCTVRIEESS
She'll play a role—in this.

‾ ‾ ‾ ‾ ‾ ‾ ‾ ‾ — ‾ ‾ ‾ ‾ ‾

3. PAWAINTLELR
He'll apply a color—to this.

‾ ‾ ‾ ‾ ‾ ‾ ‾ — ‾ ‾ ‾ ‾

4. WAFITOEORD
He'll serve you—by bringing you this.

‾ ‾ ‾ ‾ ‾ ‾ — ‾ ‾ ‾ ‾

5. DOHOCSTOPRITAL
She'll treat your ailment—at this.

‾ ‾ ‾ ‾ ‾ ‾ — ‾ ‾ ‾ ‾ ‾ ‾ ‾ ‾

6. CJOMOIKCES
He'll make you laugh—with these.

‾ ‾ ‾ ‾ ‾ — ‾ ‾ ‾ ‾ ‾

SPOT THE SPY

Which one of these secret agents is really a spy? He's the only one who is different from the rest! Find and circle the spy.

MYSTERY WORD SEARCH

Find and circle the following words having to do with baseball. The letters that remain, once listed in the order in which they appear, will spell out the mystery word.

**BALL ✦ BUNT ✦ COACH ✦ DOUBLE ✦ FIELD ✦ HIT
HOME RUN ✦ OUT ✦ PITCH ✦ SAFE ✦ STRIKE
SWING ✦ TEAMS ✦ THROW**

```
H  C  A  O  C  U  M  P
C  O  T  H  R  O  W  F
T  U  M  I  H  I  T  I
I  T  T  E  A  M  S  E
P  E  K  I  R  T  S  L
R  E  E  L  B  U  O  D
E  F  A  S  W  I  N  G
B  U  N  T  L  L  A  B
```

Mystery word: __ __ __ __ __ __

PICTURE CROSSWORD

Across

3.

4.

6.

7.

Down

1.

2.

3.

5.

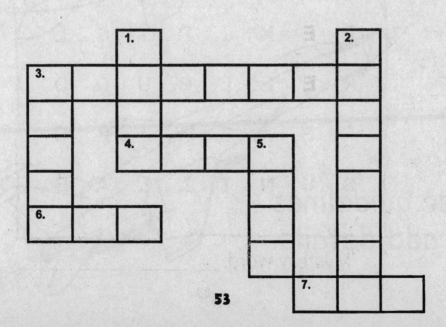

DRAW AN F-14 TOMCAT

1. Lightly draw the basic shapes.

2. Add shapes over the figure you created in step #1.

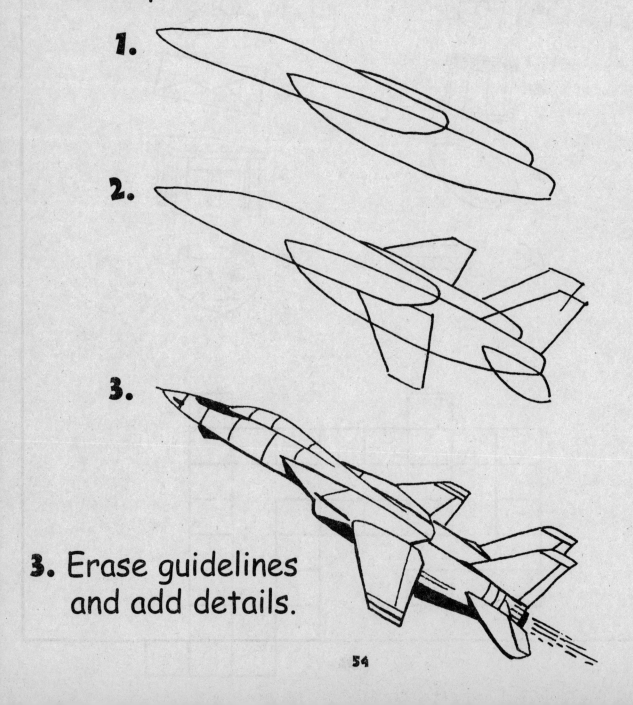

1.

2.

3.

3. Erase guidelines and add details.

Draw your F-14 here.

WHAT'S WRONG HERE?

Find and circle **10** things that are wrong or don't belong in this 19th-century Wild West scene.

DETECTIVE DECODER

There is a special note for you below—but it's in code! Decode the message using this special chart.

A=12	D=3	E=10	F=6
H=14	I=8	L=4	N=11
O=7	P=1	R=15	S=9
T=5	U=16	V=13	Y=2

$\frac{}{8}\ \frac{}{5}$ $\frac{}{3}\ \frac{}{7}\ \frac{}{10}\ \frac{}{9}\ \frac{}{11}$ '$\frac{}{5}$

$\frac{}{1}\ \frac{}{12}\ \frac{}{2}$ $\frac{}{5}\ \frac{}{7}$

$\frac{}{4}\ \frac{}{8}\ \frac{}{13}\ \frac{}{10}$ $\frac{}{8}\ \frac{}{11}$ $\frac{}{5}\ \frac{}{14}\ \frac{}{10}$

$\frac{}{1}\ \frac{}{12}\ \frac{}{9}\ \frac{}{5}$ ... $\frac{}{5}\ \frac{}{14}\ \frac{}{10}\ \frac{}{15}\ \frac{}{10}$ '$\frac{}{9}$

$\frac{}{11}\ \frac{}{7}$ $\frac{}{6}\ \frac{}{16}\ \frac{}{5}\ \frac{}{16}\ \frac{}{15}\ \frac{}{10}$

$\frac{}{8}\ \frac{}{11}$ $\frac{}{8}\ \frac{}{5}$!

UFO ADVENTURE MAZE

Two friendly aliens from Mars have accidentally entered our atmosphere! Can you help their ship return to its home planet without making any unnecessary encounters? Travel through this multipage maze to find out.

ROSWELL, NEW MEXICO

Help this flying saucer go undetected by correctly traveling through this maze of letters. Choose the path made up of the letters **U**, **F**, and **O** only!
(Move vertically or horizontally only.)

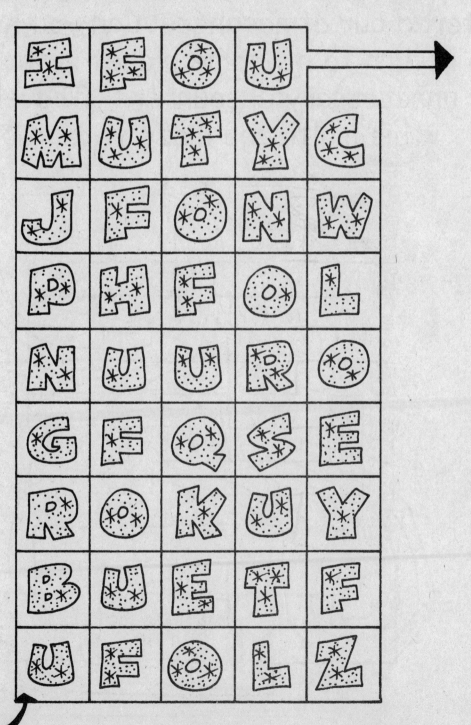

There are many places that these space travelers would love to stop and visit, but don't let them!

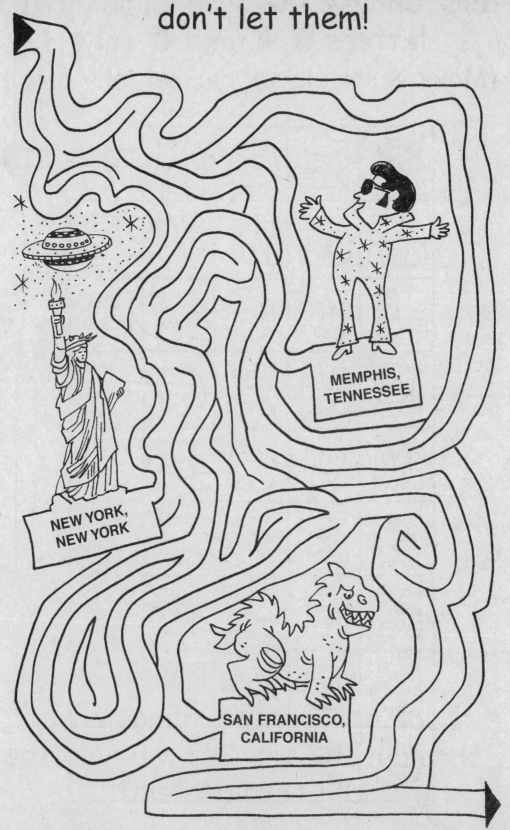

NEW YORK, NEW YORK

MEMPHIS, TENNESSEE

SAN FRANCISCO, CALIFORNIA

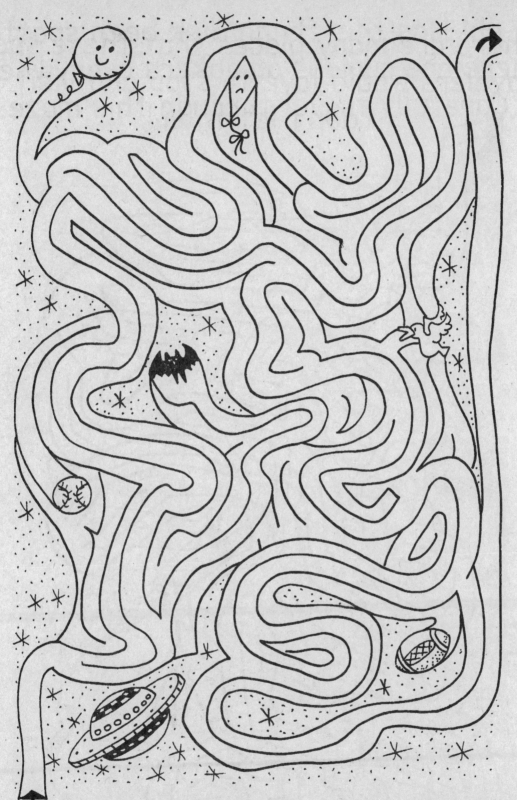

Look at all these things flying through the air! Can you help the UFO avoid them?

Uh-oh! Has this flying disk been spotted? There are curious onlookers everywhere! Carefully travel through this maze.

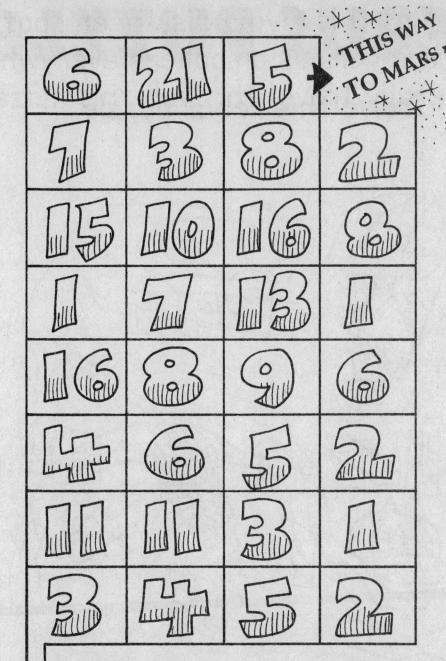

The aliens are almost back on track! Help them reach outer space by choosing the path made up only of **ODD** numbers. Farewell space visitors. See you on Mars! (Move vertically or horizontally only.)

REBUS PUZZLE

Solve this rebus puzzle.

= _ _ _ _ _ _ _ _ _ _

TAKE A LOOK

Carefully study this picture for as long as you like. Then turn the page and answer the questions without looking back at this page.

TEST YOUR MEMORY

Don't look back at the picture!

1. How many people are waiting for the elevator?
2. What floor are they on?
3. How many people are wearing hats?
4. What time is it?
5. Is anyone pushing the up button?
6. Is anyone carrying a football?
7. How many people are wearing eyeglasses?
8. Did someone drop a pencil?
9. Is anyone holding flowers?
10. Is anyone playing with a yo-yo?
11. Did someone fall asleep?
12. Is anyone pushing the down button?

JUST THE OPPOSITE

Write the opposite of each word in the spaces to the right. Then place the numbered letters below to complete the sentence.

EAST
$\overline{}_{7}\ \overline{}_{15}\ \overline{}_{5}\ \overline{}_{9}$

SLOW
$\overline{}_{12}\ \overline{}_{13}\ \overline{}_{17}\ \overline{}_{6}$

LATE
$\overline{}_{16}\ \overline{}_{8}\ \overline{}_{11}\ \overline{}_{3}$

HOT
$\overline{}_{19}\ \overline{}_{2}\ \overline{}_{14}\ \overline{}_{4}$

DRY
$\overline{}_{1}\ \overline{}_{10}\ \overline{}_{18}$

THE __ R __ 'S
    1 2   3 4

HIGHE __ __   __ __ __ __ __ __ __ __ L
      5 6   7 8 9 10 11 12 13 14

IS IN V __ N __ ZUELA,
       15   16

__ OU __ H AMERI __ A.
17   18   19

67

ALL AROUND THE WORLD WORD SEARCH

- ☐ BELGIUM
- ☐ BULGARIA
- ☐ ENGLAND
- ☐ FRANCE
- ☐ GERMANY
- ☐ GREECE
- ☐ HUNGARY
- ☐ ITALY
- ☐ JAPAN
- ☐ MEXICO
- ☐ POLAND
- ☐ SPAIN

```
J G Y R A G N U H
S D N A L O P V P
F R A N C E T C L
G K M U I G L E B
R N R Y L A T I J
E J E P R Y P L T
E N G L A N D S O
C M R O C I X E M
E A I R A G L U B
J A P A N G S A U
```

HOLIDAY PIX CROSSWORD

MYSTERY PICTURE

Draw exactly what you see in the numbered boxes at the top into the blank boxes of the same number below.

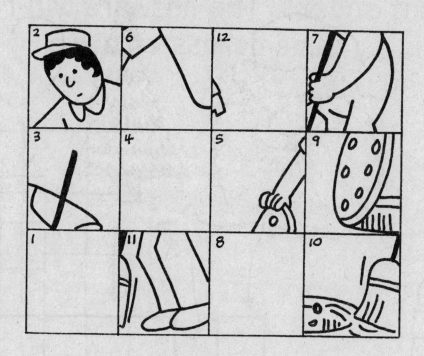

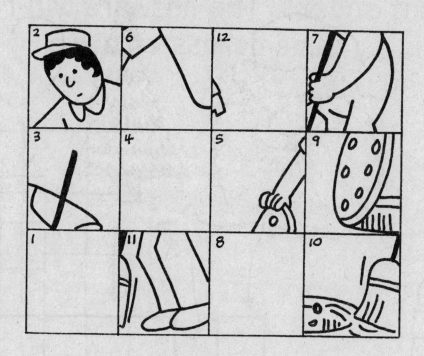

EACH WAY PUZZLES

Answer these clues and write them in their correct spaces. The answers will read the same across or down.

1. Long-tailed rodent ①

2. What we breathe ②

3. To make an effort ③

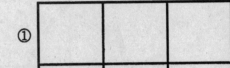

---

1. Large ①

2. Frozen water ②

3. A precious stone ③

A MUSICAL CROSSWORD

ACROSS
2. One who writes music
4. __, re, mi, fa
5. Stringed instrument
7. The speed of a piece of music

DOWN
1. Brass instrument
2. Beethoven's music
3. Rock 'n' _____
6. Woodwind instrument
8. Keyboard instrument

DETECTIVE DECODER

Using the chart below, decode this historical fact.

	A	B	C	D	E	F	G
1.	N	T	B	U	C	M	F
2.	I	D	P	S	R	A	Q
3.	V	Y	H	O	L	E	G

2C 3F 1A 1A 2D 3B 3E 3A 2F 1A 2A 2F

1C 3F 1E 2F 1F 3F   1B 3C 3F

2D 3F 1E 3D 1A 2B   1D. 2D.

2D 1B 2F 1B 3F   2A 1A

2B 3F 1E 3F 1F 1C 3F 2E   3D 1G

1787.

SEARCH & FIND®

HOME VIDEO FUN?

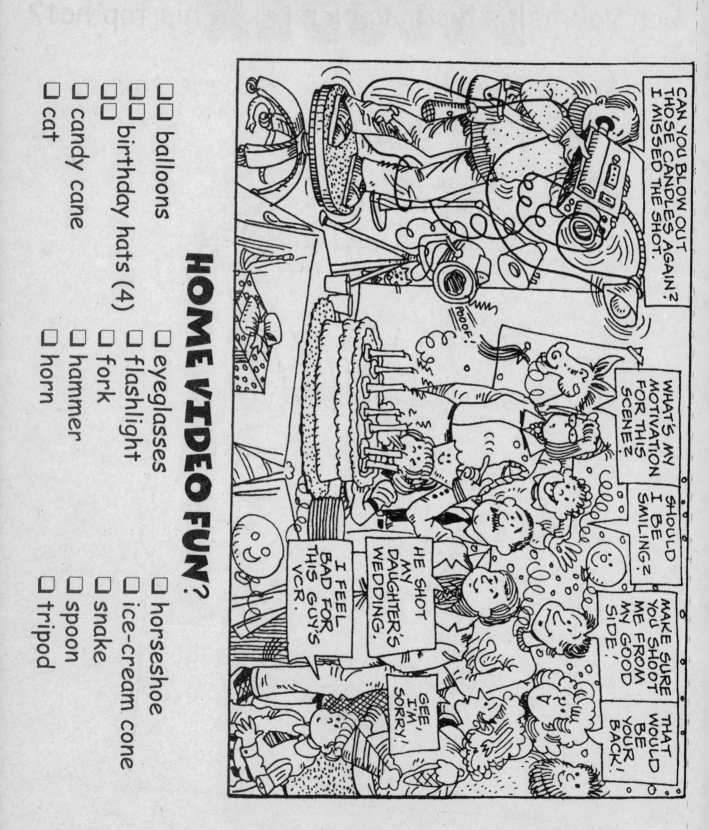

- [ ] balloons
- [ ] birthday hats (4)
- [ ] candy cane
- [ ] cat
- [ ] eyeglasses
- [ ] flashlight
- [ ] fork
- [ ] hammer
- [ ] horn
- [ ] horseshoe
- [ ] ice-cream cone
- [ ] snake
- [ ] spoon
- [ ] tripod

TOP HAT MAZE

Can you help this magician reach his top hat?

ROUND AND ROUND

These word wheels can spell hidden names! Start with the number one, go twice around the circle clockwise, and write every other letter in the spaces below.

Published the first American dictionary

_ _ _ _ _

_ _ _ _ _ _ _ _

Olympic swimming champion

_ _ _ _

_ _ _ _ _

ON THE LOOKOUT

How many things can you find in this scene that begin with the letter **H**? Circle them.

DROPPING LETTERS

Drop a letter from every word in column **A** to complete the new word in column **B**. Write each dropped letter in column **C** to form a mystery word.

	A	B	C
	STARE	_ _ T _	_ _ _ _
	WEST	_ E _	_ _ _ _
	INTO	_ O _	_ _ _ _
	MEET	_ E _	_ _ _ _
	SAME	_ E _	_ _ _ _
	DINE	_ _ D	_ _ _ _
	NEST	_ E _	_ _ _ _
	GROW	_ _ W	_ _ _ _

ANSWERS TO PUZZLES

	E	G	G		
B	I	G	G	E	R
G	A	R	A	G	E
T	A	G	G	E	D
W	I	G	G	L	E
G	I	G	G	L	E
G	A	R	G	L	E

G	E	T	T	I	N	G
G	E	O	L	O	G	Y

G	O	R	G	E	O	U	S
L	E	G	G	I	N	G	S
G	R	E	E	T	I	N	G

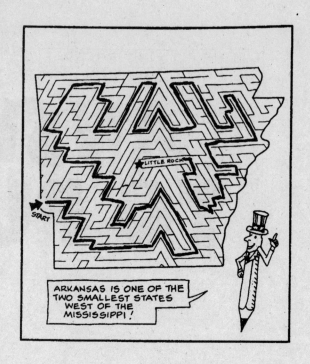

ARKANSAS IS ONE OF THE TWO SMALLEST STATES WEST OF THE MISSISSIPPI!

M E R C U R Y   I S
C1 A4 B6 B2 C5 B6 A1   A6 C2

T H E   P L A N E T
A2 C6 A4   B1 B3 C3 A3 A4 A2

C L O S E S T   T O
B2 B3 C4 C2 A4 C2 A2   A2 C4

T H E   S U N
A2 B4 A4   C2 C5 A3

= SUSPENDERS

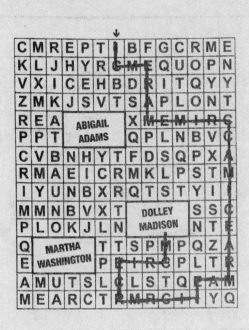

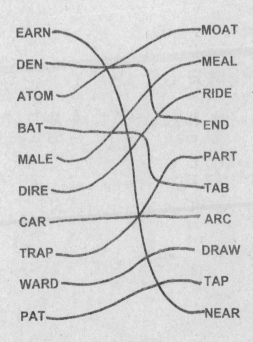

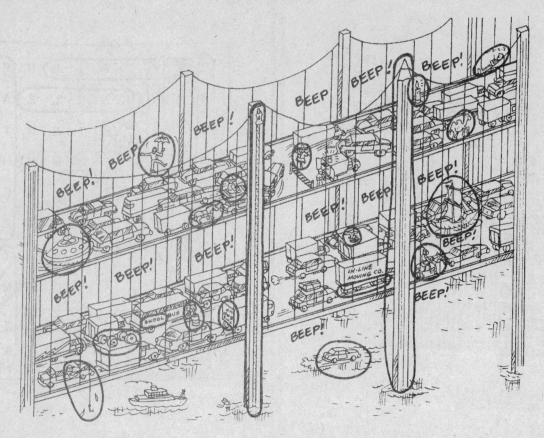

PAGE 16

PAGE 17

1. Your eyes enable you to
   SEA or (SEE)

2. A vegetable related to the onion is a
   (LEEK) or LEAK .

3. A preserve made of fruit is called
   (JAM) or JAMB .

4. You wear sneakers on your
   (FEET) or FEAT .

5. A fruit with a rounded base is a
   (PEAR) or PAIR .

6. A part in a play is called a
   ROLL or (ROLE) .

PAGE 18

Across

①
④
⑥
⑦

Down

①
②
③
⑤

①L	I	②G	H	T	B	U	L	B
O		H			③R			
B		O			R			
S		S		④C	O	W	B	O	Y
T		T			M			W	
E|						|⑥L|E|A|F
⑦R	A	D	I	O				

PAGE 19

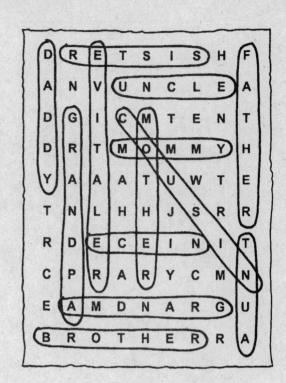

```
D R E T S I S H F
A N V U N C L E A
D G I C M T E N T
D R T M O M M Y H
Y A A T U W T E
T N L H H J S R R
R D E C E I N I T
C P R A R Y C M N
E A M D N A R G U
B R O T H E R R A
```

PAGE 20

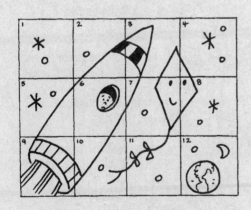

PAGE 21

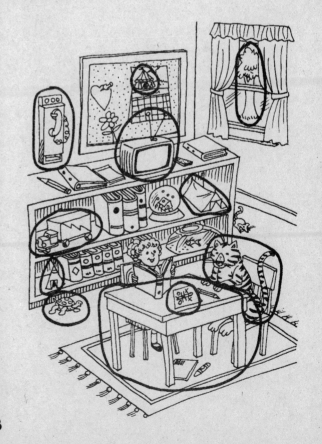

83

A	B	C
NEST	NET	S
OUR	OR	U
HER	HE	R
SIFT	SIT	F
RAIN	RAN	I
NONE	ONE	N
GROW	ROW	G

A=14
C=9
D=11
E=6
F=16
H=2
I=13
K=7
M=5
N=12
O=3
P=10
S=1
T=15
U=8
W=4
X=17

WHAT KIND
4 2 14 15   7 13 12 11

OF PHONE
3 16   10 2 3 12 6

CAN MAKE
9 14 12   5 14 7 6

MUSIC?
5 8 1 13 9

A
14

SAXOPHONE!
1 14 17 3 10 2 3 12 6

HA-HA-HA   -HA-HA-   HA-HA-HA!

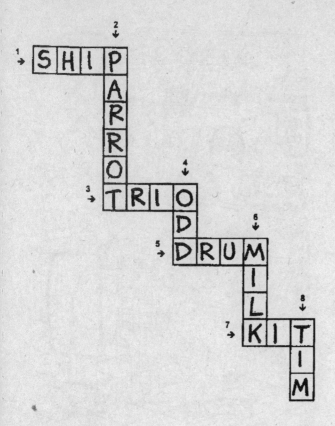

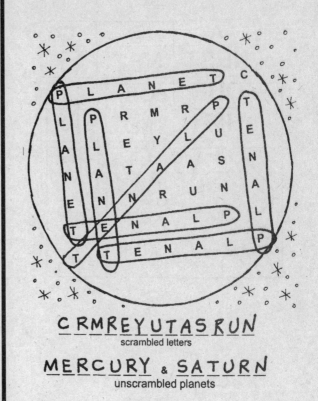

CRMREYUTAS RUN
scrambled letters

MERCURY & SATURN
unscrambled planets

PAGE 30

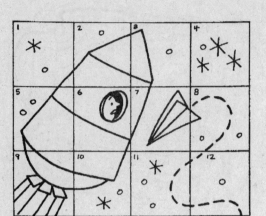

PAGE 31

PAGE 32

V E S T

P I E

C A R

D O G

K I T E

O N E

B I R D

B A L L

PAGE 33

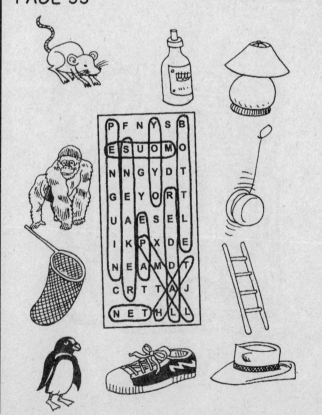

A-	3, 6, 12, 24, 48,	96
B-	22, 20, 18, 16, 14,	12
C-	35, 40, 45, 50, 55,	60
D-	30, 34, 38, 42, 46,	50
E-	1, 3, 5, 7, 9,	11
F-	71, 72, 73, 74, 75,	76
G-	15, 25, 35, 45, 55,	65

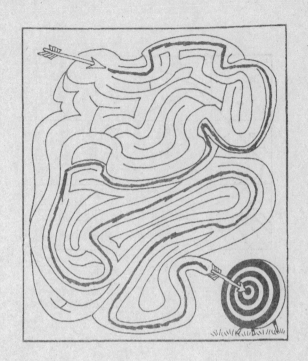

THE ANCIENT
U I F   B O D J F O U

CITY OF
D J U Z   P G

POMPEII, ITALY,
Q P N Q F J J   J U B M Z

WAS BURIED
X B T   C V S J F E

UNDER ASH AND
V O E F S   B T I   B O E

ROCK WHEN THE
S P D L   X I F O   U I F

VOLCANO
W P M D B O P

MT. VESUVIUS
N U   W F T V W J V T

ERUPTED IN 79 A.D.

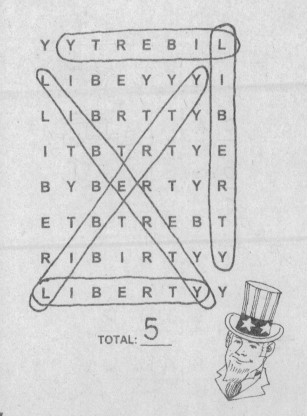

TOTAL: 5

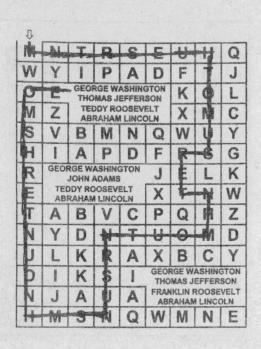

M N T R S E U H Q

W Y I P A D F T J

O E **GEORGE WASHINGTON** K O L
THOMAS JEFFERSON

M Z **TEDDY ROOSEVELT** X N C
ABRAHAM LINCOLN

S V B M N Q W U Y

H I A P D F R S G

R E **GEORGE WASHINGTON** J E L K
JOHN ADAMS

E T **TEDDY ROOSEVELT** X F N W
ABRAHAM LINCOLN

E T A B V C P Q H Z

N Y D N T U O M D

U L K R A X B C Y

D I K S I **GEORGE WASHINGTON**
THOMAS JEFFERSON

N J A U A **FRANKLIN ROOSEVELT**
ABRAHAM LINCOLN

H M S N Q W M N E

W H A T I S T H E
13 9 7 16 18 10 16 9 11

M O S T
12 17 10 16

D I F F I C U L T
1 18 5 5 18 14 2 15 16

K E Y T O T U R N ?
3 11 6 16 17 16 2 4 8

A
7

D O N K E Y !
1 17 8 3 11 6

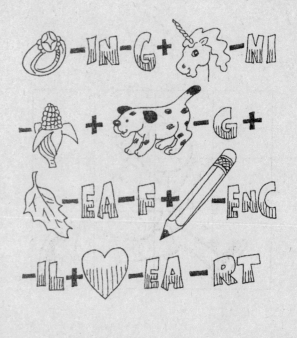

HEE-HAW!

=RUDOLPH

PAGE 44

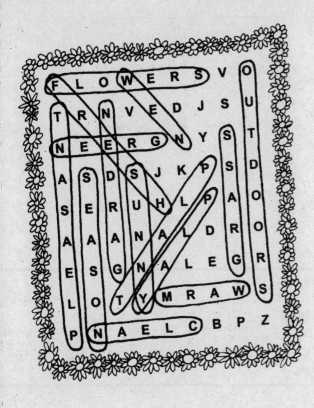

PAGE 45

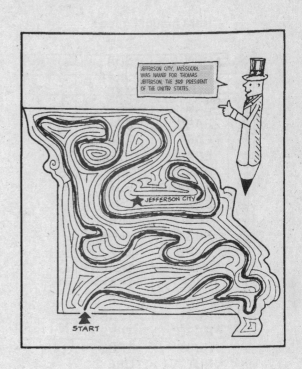

PAGE 46

PAGE 47

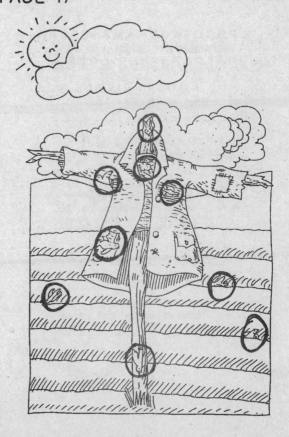

Here are just a few:

ARE	SAT
ART	SEA
ASTER	SEAT
ATE	SEE
EAR	SET
EASE	STAR
EAST	STARE
ERA	STEER
ERASE	SUE
ERASURE	SUET
ERE	SURE
ERR	TAR
ERST	TARE
RARE	TEA
RAT	TEAR
RATE	TEASE
REAR	TEE
REST	TERSE
RUSE	TREE
RUST	TRUE
RUT	USE

Sport played on a court
B A S K E T B A L L
18 12 13   6   1

Medical expert   D O C T O R
                  4   7   17

Opposite of over   U N D E R
                   14 9 11   20

Long-necked mammal   G I R A F F E
                     5 3 10   16

Spring month A P R I L
              8 15 2 19

THE FIRST B R I D G E TO   C A N A D A
          1 2 3 4 5 6   7 8 9 10 11 12

WAS A   S U S P E N S I O N   BRIDGE
        13 14 15 16   17

B UILT FROM N I A G A R A FALLS, NEW YORK.
18   19   20

1. **PHCOTAOGRAMPHERERA**
He'll snap your picture - with this
P H O T O G R A P H E R - C A M E R A

2. **AMOCTVRIEESS**
She'll play a role - in this
A C T R E S S - M O V I E

3. **PAWAINTLELR**
He'll apply a color - to this
P A I N T E R - W A L L

4. **WAFITOEORD**
He'll serve you - by bringing you this
W A I T E R - F O O D

5. **DOHOCSTOPRITAL**
She'll treat your ailment - at this
D O C T O R - H O S P I T A L

6. **CJOMOIKCES**
He'll make you laugh - with these
C O M I C - J O K E S

PAGE 52

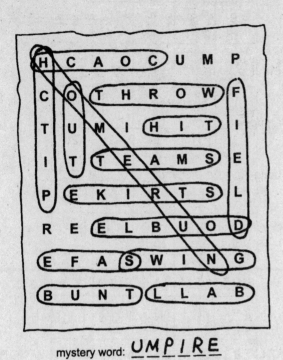

```
H C A O C U M P
C O T H R O W F
T U M I H I T I
I T T E A M S E
P E K I R T S L
R E E L B U O D
E F A S W I N G
B U N T L L A B
```

mystery word: <u>U M P I R E</u>

PAGE 53

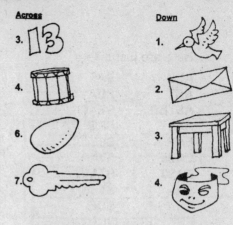

3. 13
4. (drum)
6. (egg)
7. (key)

1. (bird)
2. (envelope)
3. (table)
4. (mask)

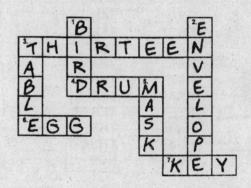

Crossword solution:

```
          B           E
  T H I R T E E N     N
  A     R             V
  B     D R U M       E
  L         A         L
  E G G     S         O
            K         P
              K E Y
```

ABLE (down), BIRD (down), THIRTEEN (across), DRUM (across), MASK (down), ENVELOPE (down), EGG (across), KEY (across)

PAGE 56

PAGE 57

IT DOESN'T
8 5   3 7 10 9 11 5

PAY TO
1 12 2   5 7

LIVE IN THE
4 8 13 10   8 11   5 14 10

PAST ... THERE'S
1 12 9 5   5 14 10 15 10 9

NO FUTURE
11 7   6 16 5 16 15 10

IN IT!
8 11   8 5

PAGE 58

PAGE 59

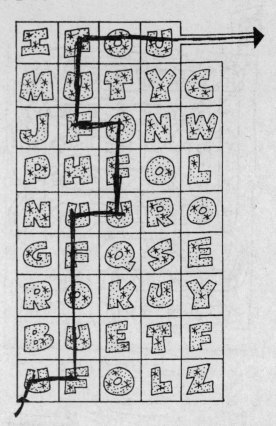

PAGE 60

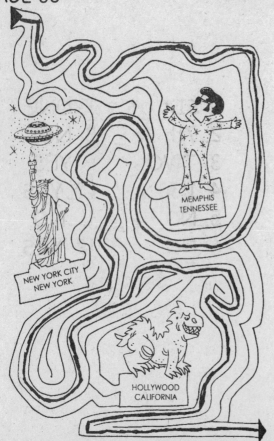

PAGE 61

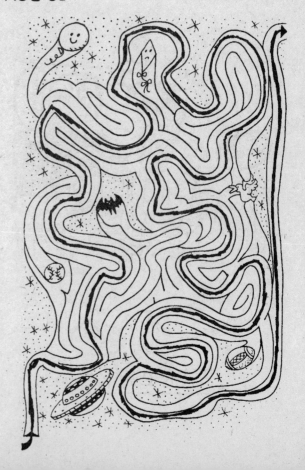

PAGE 62

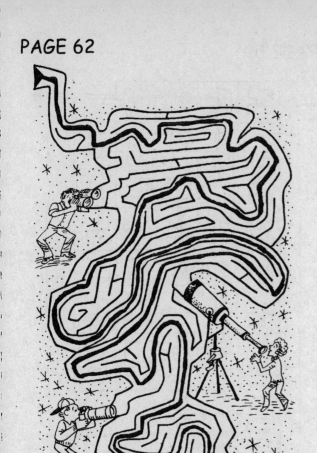

PAGE 63

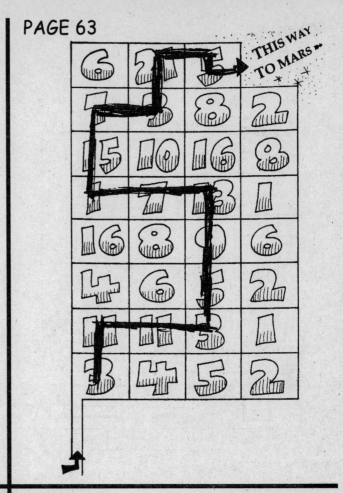

THIS WAY TO MARS

PAGE 64

- RAC

- HUTE + - ET

+ - P + - Y

+ - H - OE

= P A N C A K E S

PAGE 66

1. SIX	7. ONE
2. 7th	8. NO
3. TWO	9. YES
4. 1:30	10. YES
5. NO	11. NO
6. NO	12. YES

PAGE 67

EAST	W E S T
	7 15 5 9
SLOW	F A S T
	12 13 17 6
LATE	E A R L Y
	16 8 11 3
HOT	C O L D
	19 2 14 4
DRY	W E T
	1 10 18

THE W O r L D 's
    1 2 3 4

HIGHE S T   W A T E R F A L L
      5 6 7 8 9 10 11 12 13 14

IS IN V E N E ZUELA,
      15 16

S OU T H AMERI C A.
17 18   19

PAGE 68

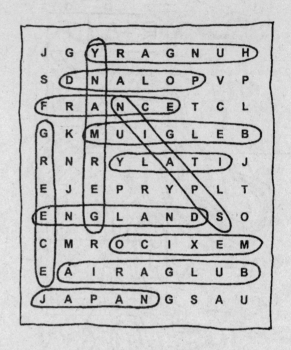

PAGE 69

PAGE 70

94

1. Long-tailed rodent

2. What we breathe

3. To make an effort

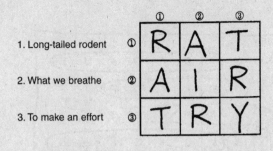

	①	②	③
①	R	A	T
②	A	I	R
③	T	R	Y

1. Large

2. Frozen water

3. A precious stone

	①	②	③
①	B	I	G
②	I	C	E
③	G	E	M

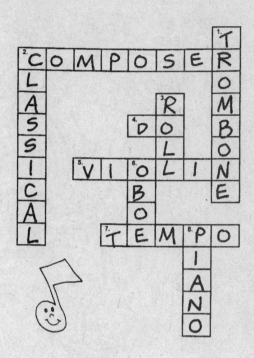

PENNSYLVANIA
2C 3F 1A 1A 2D 3B 3E 3A 2F 1A 2A 2F

BECAME THE
1C 3F 1E 2F 1F 3F   1B 3C 3F

SECOND U.S.
2D 3F 1E 3D 1A 2B   1D 2D

STATE IN
2D 1B 2F 1B 3F   2A 1A

DECEMBER OF
2B 3F 1E 3F 1F 1C 3F 2E   3D 1G

1787.

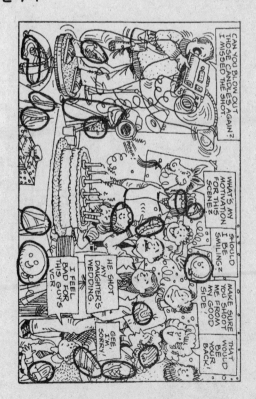

PAGE 75

START

PAGE 76

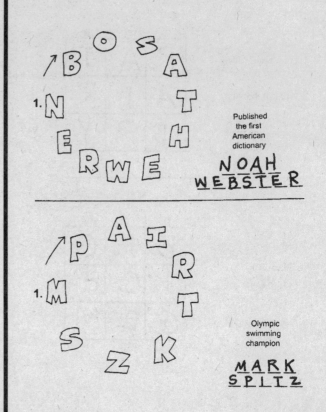

1. B O S A T H

N E R W E H

Published the first American dictionary

NOAH WEBSTER

1. P A I R T

M S Z K

Olympic swimming champion

MARK SPITZ

PAGE 77

PAGE 78

	A	B	C
STARE	R A T E	S
WEST	S E T	W
INTO	N O T	I
MEET	T E E	M
SAME	S E A	M
DINE	E N D	I
NEST	S E T	N
GROW	R O W	G